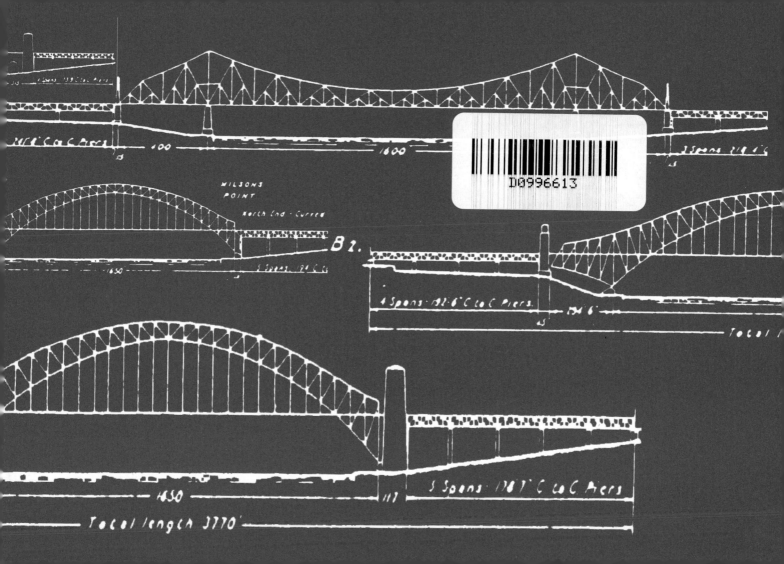

WILSONS
POINT

North End - Curved

B 2.

4 Spans · 192'6" C to C Piers.

134'6"

1650

5 Spans · 94 C to C

Total l

100

1600

3 Spans 110 C to C

1450

111

5 Spans · 198'7" C to C. Piers

Total length 3770'

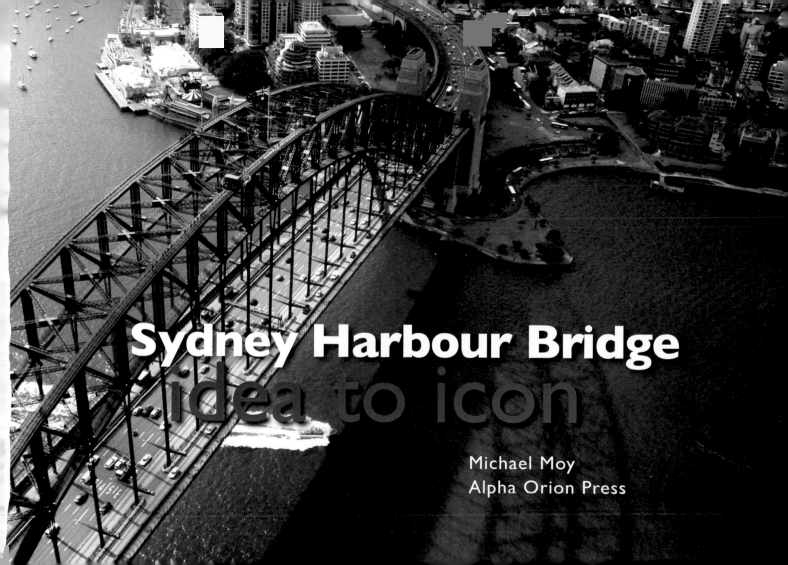

Sydney Harbour Bridge
idea to icon

Michael Moy
Alpha Orion Press

... There shall broad streets their stately walls extend,
The circus widen, and the crescent bend;
There, rayed from cities o'er the cultured land,
Shall bright canals, and solid roads expand.
There the proud arch, colossus-like, bestride
Yon glittering streams, and bound the chasing tide ...

From the poem, *Visit of Hope to Sydney Cove*, near Botany Bay
by Erasmus Darwin, grandfather of Charles Darwin, 1791

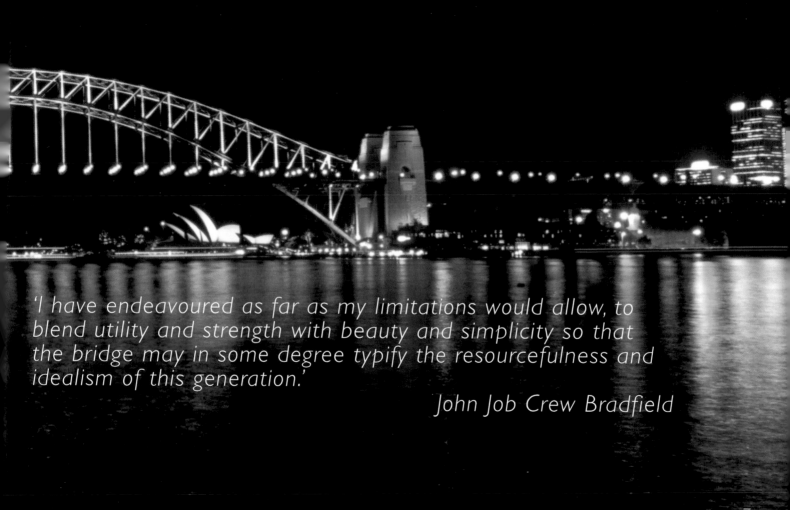

'I have endeavoured as far as my limitations would allow, to blend utility and strength with beauty and simplicity so that the bridge may in some degree typify the resourcefulness and idealism of this generation.'

John Job Crew Bradfield

Dawes Point from Bennelong Point, 1870

Sydney Cove

European settlement of Australia commenced on 26 January 1788 when the commander of the First Fleet, Captain Arthur Phillip, raised the Union Jack at Sydney Cove deep inside what he described as 'the finest harbour in the world'. Over the next few days, the seven hundred and thirty convicts exiled from England for mostly petty crime, went about unloading provisions, clearing land and erecting shelters under the guard of the British marines. A prefabricated canvas Government House was set up for Phillip to the east of what became known as the Tank Stream with convict accommodation to the west in the area now known as The Rocks. The activities were watched from a distance by an unknown number of Cadigal people whose lives would never be the same again.

TOLL CHARGE $3·00 ALL VEHICLES
NO CHANGE GIVEN AT AUTO BOOTHS

13

The great asset becomes a great obstacle

By the time the last convict ship arrived in 1840, Sydney was a thriving settlement attracting, as it has ever since, free settlers eager to start a new life. In that year, a rail line was opened on the North Shore linking St Leonards to Milsons Point, just a short walk or tram ride from a cross-harbour ferry terminal.

As the city grew to the north and south, Sydney's greatest asset, its harbour, became its greatest obstacle. The transportation of heavy freight from one side to the other involved a day-long fifty kilometre journey via Parramatta. The journey was cut in half in the 1880s with the completion of the route of five bridges: Pyrmont, Glebe Island, Iron Cove, Gladesville and Fig Tree.

Over the years there were many proposals to link north and south including a massive suspension bridge, a pontoon bridge, a cable tramway tunnel, and a causeway built from rock excavated to create a shipping canal between Neutral Bay and Lavender Bay. For reasons of poor design, lack of money, or change in government, none of these proposals got very far. The possibility of a crossing looked promising in 1900 when the Government of New South Wales advertised internationally for tenders for the design and construction of a North Shore bridge. Twenty-four submissions were received from America, Europe and Australia, prizes were awarded but none of the tenders was accepted. A year later, the government invited a second round of tenders as investigative work on the feasibility of the project continued. In 1903, a technique using a pressurised working chamber called a caisson was implemented to determine the nature of the harbour floor for possible pier installation. Pressure inside the chamber to keep water out was provided by an air pump on the surface while a blade around the base of the caisson sealed it to the harbour floor allowing the men inside to excavate what was found to be a deep layer of unstable clay above bedrock. At 4 am on 1 September, George Clark and two co-workers emerged from the caisson at the end of their shift, all feeling unwell. Two hours later, George was dead, the cause recorded as 'over-pressure of air', a condition now commonly known as the bends. The bridge had claimed its first life.

1892.

Circular Quay and future bridge site, 1892

In 1903, after lengthy consideration of the twelve submissions received in the second round of tenders, the government accepted a cantilever design, after rejecting arch proposals as too big and ugly. A short time later, to the frustration of everyone involved, a new government scrapped the project entirely.

By 1908 the ferry traffic across the harbour had become chaotic with thirteen million passenger crossings a year. Many predicted a tragedy, and a tragedy did occur, but not until 3 November 1927. At 4:30 pm that day, the steamship *Tahiti* enroute to San Francisco and the ferry *Greycliffe* bound for Vaucluse collided near Bradleys Head. The ferry sank immediately with the loss of thirty-six lives including several children who were on their way home from school.

Abandoned vehicular ferry
ramp, McMahons Point

18

The visionary

Born in 1867 at Sandgate just north of Brisbane, the son of an immigrant brickmaker, John Job Crew Bradfield studied engineering at the University of Sydney before returning to Brisbane to a position with Queensland Railways where he designed his first bridge, a footbridge at Roma Street Railway Station. Retrenched from Queensland Railways in 1891 due to an economic downturn, Bradfield returned to Sydney as a draughtsman with the New South Wales Public Works Department where he rose quickly through the ranks. Assignments early in his career included determining the viability of designs submitted in the harbour bridge tenders of the early 1900s and the design of a number of steel bridges for the West Maitland to South Grafton railway line. A resident of Gordon on Sydney's North Shore, young John Bradfield was well aware of the need for a harbour bridge. Day after day, year after year, he would travel by train to Milsons Point and then catch a ferry to his city office. He would be in his sixty-fifth year before the journey could be made by train alone.

In 1913, one year after being appointed Chief Engineer Metropolitan Railway Construction and Sydney Harbour Bridge, Bradfield submitted a proposal for the construction of a cantilever bridge from Dawes Point to Milsons Point with four rail lines in addition to a road and footways. The future of the bridge and associated railway project seemed assured when, in 1914, the Government of New South Wales sent him on a study tour of underground railways and long-span, high-level bridges in North America and Europe. In New York, Bradfield visited the Hell Gate Bridge worksite, an experience he would not forget. At 298 m long, this metal railway bridge across the East River was to be the largest arch bridge in the world. World War I broke out just weeks after Bradfield arrived in England prompting the forty-seven-year-old to volunteer for military service. Rejected by the British military, Bradfield returned to Sydney and put forward plans for the electrification of the railway system and the construction of, amongst other lines, a city loop and a line from The Domain to Bondi Junction. His civil projects shelved for the duration of the war, Bradfield involved himself in several military projects including the establishment of the New South Wales State Aviation School for the training of military pilots.

In April 1920, a Labor government under Premier John Storey was elected with a will to undertake major projects to employ and increase the skill level of returned servicemen. The bridge project was back on the table. Sydney in 1920 had a population of one million with about one-third living on the north side of the harbour. Storey's sudden death in office, a political crisis and the reconsideration of a cross-harbour tube in the light of untested, and as far as Bradfield was concerned, bogus technology slowed the process. In December 1921, the Labor government under Storey's successor, James Dooley, called for worldwide tenders for the construction of

a cantilever bridge. Early the next year, Bradfield left Australia to study the latest in bridge engineering and assure potential tenderers in Europe and North America that, this time, the Government of New South Wales meant business.

A dangerous business

In Canada, Bradfield spent hours climbing over the recently completed Québec Bridge, checking vibration with passing trains. Two failures during construction of this bridge demonstrate the dangers inherent in bridge building. The first collapse occurred in 1907 as the suspended span was being built out from a cantilever span. Just minutes before the end of the work day, two compression chords on an anchor arm failed and, in a matter of seconds, 18,000 tonne of steel thundered into the St Lawrence River killing seventy-five of the eighty-six workers on that part of the bridge.

Nine years and a Royal Commission later, Québec Bridge was once again nearing completion when another tragedy occurred. The complete suspended span was being hoisted from the river below when a steel casting failure caused it to drop, killing eleven workers. A modification in the jacking system saw a new suspended span lifted safely into place in 1917.

On the run and a change of mind

During Bradfield's overseas tour, the New South Wales Labor government lost an election to a Nationalist-Progressive coalition. The new premier, who was opposed to the bridge, ordered that a cable be sent to Bradfield in New York instructing him to go no further until the bridge matter was sorted out. Bradfield's secretary in Sydney, Kathleen Butler, was told of the order and immediately cabled her boss who vacated his lodgings and boarded a ship for England, thereby avoiding the unwelcome directive.

In England, the Cleveland Bridge Company requested Bradfield's permission to tender for an arch design, which they claimed, with modern steel, would be lighter and cheaper to build than a cantilever bridge. Bradfield also met with Georges Imbault who had built the inverted arch Victoria Falls Bridge across the Zambezi River in Africa using cable restraints to hold back the incomplete arch sections, the technique eventually used in Sydney. In addition, Bradfield heard several laudatory reports of the Hell Gate Bridge in New York which he had inspected during construction. Whatever it was that convinced him to change his mind, Bradfield cabled Sydney to have the arch possibility added to the tender documentation and on the voyage home worked long hours drawing up the necessary specifications, which, he found, would save £400,000 (£1, one pound, became $2 when decimal currency was introduced in Australia in 1966).

An ace up his sleeve

Bradfield arrived back in Sydney to find the new government proposing that bridge contractors be paid with toll revenue, a totally unacceptable proposition for the companies he had visited. Fortunately, Bradfield had an ace up his sleeve. North Shore residents, partly at Bradfield's instigation, had agreed to a special tax to help pay for the bridge. Should things grind to a halt again, the government would have to answer to them. On 24 November 1922, legislation enabling the construction of the bridge was passed.

Hell Gate Bridge across East River, New York, 298 m span, opened 1916. Designer: Gustav Lindenthal

Victoria Falls Bridge across Africa's Zambezi River,
157 m span, opened 1905. Designer: Ralph Freeman;
Resident Engineer: Georges Imbault

Cantilever vision, 1918

Patriotic drawing commissioned by Bradfield in 1924 with bridge decorated to resemble Australian Commonwealth Military Forces badge

The winning tender

After initiating the inclusion of an arch design in the tendering process, the Cleveland Bridge Company withdrew from the competition upon the death of their managing director. Cleveland Bridge's Ralph Freeman, who had been working on the tender for some time, asked his employer's permission to take his designs to Dorman Long and Company. Cleveland Bridge agreed and, with only four months to go until the close of tenders, Dorman Long welcomed Freeman on board.

Twenty designs from a total of six companies were received by the close of tenders on 16 January 1924. During the next month, Bradfield examined each of the submissions and wrote a report recommending one of the seven designs proposed by Dorman Long, a two-hinged steel arch bridge with five approach spans at each end. At £4.2 million, the design was the second cheapest, and, to Bradfield, clearly the best. Under the terms of the contract signed on 24 March 1924, working drawings were to be prepared by Dorman Long in London. Bradfield, accompanied by two of his engineers, visited Dorman Long soon after the signing to finalise design details and check calculations.

More than a bridge

On 28 July 1923, six months before tenders closed, the turning of the first sod to mark the beginning of the project occurred at the site of what is now North Sydney railway station. Large scale property resumption and demolition were undertaken in the early stages of the project to make way for the approach spans, connecting roads and railways. In all, eight hundred buildings, mostly houses rented by workers, were demolished with little or no compensation to those forced to leave. The Rocks and North Sydney were changed forever.

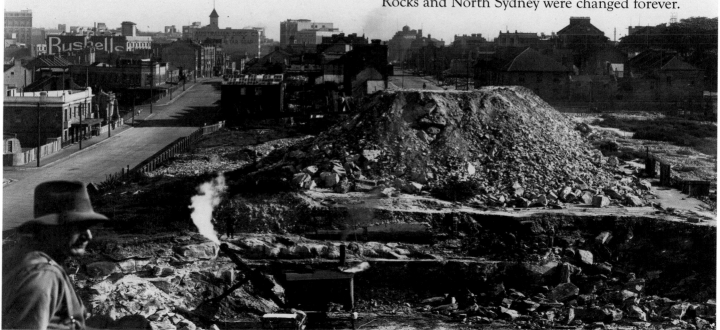

Clearing the way for the southern approach

Excavation of railway tunnel, May 1924

The quarry and workshops

Granite for the facing of the piers and pylons was quarried and cut to shape at Moruya 300 km south of Sydney and transported north in three purpose-built ships. Stonemasons were recruited in Scotland and Italy and a settlement, Granite Town, was built near the mine to house the workers and their families. Eighteen thousand cubic metres of granite facing was used on the project with waste rock used as aggregate for the bridge concrete.

Two steel fabrication workshops were built on the site of the original Milsons Point railway station, where Luna Park and the North Sydney Olympic Pool stand today. The site was widened with the excavation of 35,000 cubic metres of rock and wharves were built to accommodate ships bringing steel from Dorman Long's Middlesbrough works in England, BHP, Newcastle, and Australian Iron and Steel, Port Kembla. Dorman Long's Lawrence Ennis supervised the workshops and construction of the bridge and approaches. The shops were equipped with machines capable of straightening, cutting and drilling through metal plate up to sixty millimetres thick.

Moruya quarry site, 1927

8.
17.6.26

Dorman Long's workshops, Milsons Point

Luna Park, opened 1935

Workers with radial drills, Light Metal Workshop, Milsons Point, April 1926

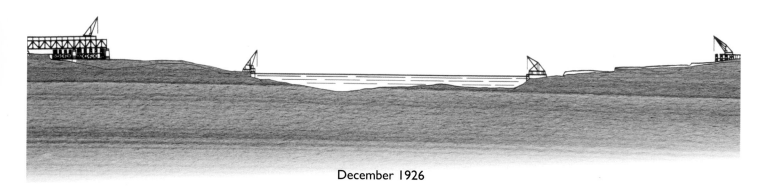

December 1926

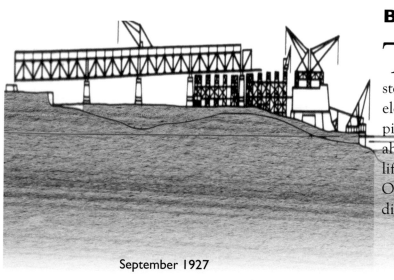

September 1927

Building the approach spans

The approach spans on both sides of the harbour were each built using two cranes, a five tonne steam locomotive crane and a twenty-five tonne electric crane. The smaller crane travelled from one pier to the next on timber falsework which it erected ahead of itself. The larger crane travelled behind lifting the steel span components onto the falsework. Once the steel span was in place, the falsework was dismantled and used to construct the next span.

5.7.27

Southern approach from George Street North, July 1927

Piers with granite facing, February 1927

Changing view outside Harbour View Hotel, July 1927

September 1928

Supporting the weight

Four 300 tonne steel bearings support the entire weight of the bridge and prevent it spreading out. The thrust on each bearing is 20,000 tonne. Since the arch sections were built out from the bearings to meet in the middle, it was vital that they were aligned precisely.

The angled foundations or skewbacks for the bearings required excavation in the sandstone to depths between nine and twelve metres, the holes being filled with concrete laid crossways in special hexagonal sections designed to provide maximum strength. Continuous pour high-grade concrete formed the base for the bearings which were aligned with the help of hydraulic jacks.

The skewbacks form part of the abutments, the large granite-faced concrete structures closest to the water on either side of the harbour. The abutments also support the final approach span on each side of the water. The expensive granite facing on the pylon concrete and the decorative towers above the roadway are testaments to Bradfield's talent as a lobbyist. He was fond of quoting John Ruskin: 'Life without industry is guilt, and industry without art is brutality.'

Excavation for skewbacks, Dawes Point, February 1926

Eastern main bearing with hydraulic jacks, Dawes Point, May 1927

Pouring concrete, southern pylon, March 1928

7
16.5.28

Southern abutment with creeper crane ramp installed on top, May 1928

The arch takes shape

In the case of Sydney Harbour Bridge, temporary arch supports in the water were not an option because of the immense size required and the hazard such supports would pose to shipping. The cable support technique implemented by Imbault and Freeman some years earlier in Africa was used to hold back the arch sections as the bridge was built out over the water. Horseshoe tunnels angled at forty-five degrees were excavated between the first and second piers on each side of the harbour, with 128 cables looped through and attached to metal plates at the ends of the top chords. The 128 cables on each side of the water each consisted of 217 individual wires with a total length of 25,600 km. Some of these restraint cables can be seen today suspending the roadway on the Walter Taylor Bridge in Brisbane and as deck hangers on the Birchenough Bridge in Zimbabwe.

Work on the arch started on 16 October 1928. Creeper cranes, each weighing 600 tonne with the capacity to lift up to 120 tonne, were assembled on temporary ramps on the top of the northern and southern abutments. The first task was to lift the first vertical member from a barge below and place it in position on top of the main bearing. That job done, the other metal components of the first panel were lifted into place and riveted together. When the first panel was complete, the crane moved onto it and the second panel was assembled just like the first. In all, there are twenty-eight panels across the length of the bridge.

November 1929

Barge crane unloads first sections of main arch at Dawes Point, October 1928. Creeper crane on abutment tower is assembled and operating

Erection of second panel of arch, May 1929

Restraining cables are clearly visible in this view from Bennelong
Point as the fourth panel nears completion, August 1929

January 1930

May 1930

Workers check tension with cables close to maximum load, August 1930, and inside horseshoe cable tunnel

Industry without art is brutality

The grand spectacle of the bridge taking shape was captured by a young Grace Cossington Smith who travelled from her Turramurra home to Milsons Point where she spent hours in the sometimes blustery conditions sketching the evolving curves and lines. *The Bridge in-curve*, rejected by the Society of Artists exhibition in 1930 and now considered one of Australia's most significant modernists paintings, and *The curve of the Bridge*, recently brought back to Australia after a sixty-year absence, belong to different galleries but were displayed together in 2006 as part of a National Gallery of Australia exhibition.

Left painting: *The Bridge in-curve*, c.1930, tempera on cardboard, National Gallery of Victoria, Melbourne

Right painting: *The curve of the Bridge*, 1928-1929, oil on cardboard, Art Gallery of New South Wales, Sydney

49

John Bradfield, Lawrence Ennis and Ennis's assistant, Clarence Hipwell, join
riveters and riggers on bottom chord, 13 August 1930

The halves meet

On the 7 August 1930, the 15,000 tonne arch halves were just under a metre apart, swinging slightly in the breeze, their lengths and consequently the gap between north and south varying with ambient temperature and amount of incident sunlight. A plank was laid across the gap with Lawrence Ennis the first to cross it. The slow, calculated slackening of the cables, now under maximum load, commenced on that day and continued around the clock for three weeks. On 12 August a storm that brought snow to the Blue Mountains descended on Sydney with winds of 110 km/h. Ennis, supremely confident that the structure would hold, recorded a swing of only forty millimetres amplitude at the top. At 4:15 pm on 19 August the two halves touched only to part a short time after sunset. With slackening continuing on the cables, the two halves touched again at 10 pm and were locked together with pins. Flags flew from the bridge the next morning signalling the success of the operation, prompting ships and ferries to sound their horns. North and south were joined at last. Workers involved in the closing were each given a gold sovereign with other workers given two shillings to toast the bridge, and half a day off to do so.

The bridge was now a three hinge arch, with a hinge at each abutment and one in the bottom chord. The next step, joining the top chord halves, was completed on 9 September with cloud providing an even temperature across the bridge. Hydraulic jacks were used to open the gaps to a specified width into which packing pieces were inserted and attached. The top chord complete, the bridge became a two hinge arch.

August 1930

1930

Hydraulic jacks open top chord gap, 8 September 1930

Hanging the deck

The next task was to suspend the deck from the arch. The deck hangers, which varied in length from fifty-nine metres in the middle of the bridge to seven metres at the ends, were lifted into position by the creeper cranes backing down the arch as the work progressed. Crossbeams were installed between the hangers and steel troughs laid on top. Low density coke concrete was poured on the troughs to a depth of 100 mm and topped with asphalt. Two railway lines were laid on the western side of the deck, one on each side of the hangers to minimise twisting force; two tramway lines were laid on the east side the same way; and pedestrian walkways were installed on both sides of the deck. A period of testing followed. One test involved monitoring deflection when the deck was loaded with ninety-two locomotives, a weight of almost 8000 tonne. The load, more than any bridge anywhere had been required to support, caused a deflection of eighty millimetres. When the locomotives were removed, the bridge resumed its shape, just like a spring.

October 1930

Lifting middle deck hanger, September 1930

Deck assembly progresses with creeper cranes backing down arch, December 1930

Load testing with locomotives

Complex task, simple tools

The enormous task of building the bridge was accomplished with equipment considered primitive by modern standards. Engineers used slide rules and cumbersome manual calculating machines to solve complex mathematical equations with dozens of variables. Safety equipment was almost non-existent. Workers wore their own clothing and sandshoes which needed replacing every couple of months. Carpenters supplied their own tools. Concrete was mixed in mixers of three-quarters of a cubic metre capacity tended by day labourers with wheelbarrows. Five-tonne motor lorries and horse-drawn carts carried materials around the site. Rivets for joining steel components on the bridge were cooked in coke or oil-fired furnaces close to where they were needed. Withdrawn from the oven with tongs, a soft, sparkling, almost white-hot rivet would be tossed to a worker who would catch it with a funnel-like device, then, using tongs, quickly place it in a pre-drilled hole where pneumatic equipment would hammer it closed. The riveting of chord components required a man inside the cramped chord to apply pressure to the hot rivet. Each rivet was subsequently checked by an inspector who, with a finger touching one end, would tap the other end with a small hammer and sense the vibration and sound. A loose rivet would give itself away and be removed. Of the five to six million rivets placed in the bridge, about 100,000 were found faulty and removed. Some were dropped into the water below prompting one commentator to quip that the bridge would soon be unnecessary as a person would be able to walk across the harbour on rivets.

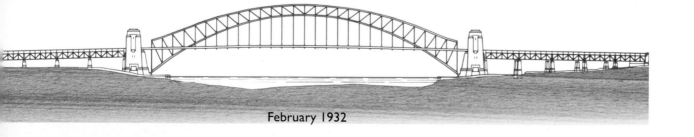

February 1932

The workers, the casualties

The average size of the workforce on the bridge during the eight years of construction was 1400 with many more employed by the various suppliers. During that time, New South Wales went from boom to bust as a result of the Great Depression. At the start of the project, preference of employment was given to war veterans and union members. Later, as the depression bit, preference went to family men. In an effort to share the available work, working hours were progressively reduced from forty-four hours per week in 1924, to thirty-three hours per week in 1931. Because of the life it breathed into the sick economy, the bridge project was christened 'The iron lung'. At the end of the project, bridge workers walked out into a world of thirty percent unemployment.

Only thirty-two days were lost to industrial action during the length of the project, mostly over safety issues. This low level of dispute was, no doubt, partly due to the economic conditions; however, some credit must go to Bradfield who had a reputation as a fair man who treated workers with respect. Bradfield had written a clause into the construction contract making the government responsible for any costs associated with wage increases. Perhaps it was because of this clause that Dorman Long supported efforts by workers to gain wage increases to compensate for the dangerous working conditions rather than improve conditions by providing nets and other safety equipment at their expense. Dorman Long's Director of Construction, Lawrence Ennis, addressed criticism of wage increases by those who 'knew all about bridge building from their armchairs and verandahs round the harbour'

Sheet asphalt plant, September 1931

by saying, 'Every day those men went onto the bridge, they went in the same way as a soldier goes into battle, not knowing whether they would come down alive or not.'

Sixteen workers lost their lives during construction and many more suffered broken limbs, severed fingers and toes, and worse. In 1926, dogman Henry Waters died from an injury in a crane accident at the Moruya quarry, and braceman Robert Craig fell down a ballast heap at Milsons Point when a hopper he was emptying tipped. In 1927, quarryman Percival Poole was crushed by falling rock at the quarry face, slinger Angel Peterson died several months after his spine was fractured by falling steel in the Milsons Point workshop, and boilermaker's assistant Nathaniel Swandells fell to his death from an approach pier. In 1928, rigger William Woods fell from the approach span at Milsons Point, and carpenter Edward Shirley died after scaffolding collapsed on him at the Fitzroy Street arch. That year saw boilermakers and ironworkers walk off the job demanding shorter shifts and higher pay for working at such dangerous heights. In 1929, rigger Thomas McKeown and three workmates were lowering the staging on which they were standing under the deck at Dawes Point when it suddenly tilted. McKeown's workmates lunged for a girder and were saved while McKeown grabbed the rapidly moving staging chain only to have his left hand and leg severed when the links he was holding reached the pulley system. He fell fifty metres to the ground. The day after this gruesome death, Judge Beeby of the Commonwealth Arbitration Court handed down a long awaited ruling granting wage increases of up to seventy-five percent for workers on the arch saying, 'A community which asks such unusual service must be prepared to offer unusual wages.'

In 1930, boilermaker's assistant Sydney Addison was tightening a nut on the north side of the arch when he fell backwards into the water sixty metres below, and Frederick Gillon was crushed by scaffolding at North Sydney. In 1931, a half-tonne metal sheet fell from a creeper crane onto the deck striking rigger John Faulkner a fatal blow, dogman James Chilvers drowned after being knocked from the workshop wharf when steel he was unloading came loose, John Webb fell while painting cross girders inside a

southern pylon, Alfred Edmunds died of tetanus eleven days after crushing his thumb packing stones, and day labourer Robert Graham was hit by a tram in Alfred Street, North Sydney.

The last death occurred in January 1932, two months before the bridge opened, when a gust of wind caused foreman rigger James Campbell to fall from scaffolding erected for the cleaning of pylon granite.

Amongst the deaths there was one story of miraculous survival. On 23 October 1930, boilermaker Vincent Roy Kelly, was working on deck scaffolding fifty-five metres above the water, when, in the process of moving his heavy pneumatic rivet gun, he stepped backwards into thin air. From his hospital bed, suffering nothing more serious than broken ribs, Kelly described how he twisted his body to enter the water almost vertically, feet first, with a hand clamped over his nose and mouth. 'I hit the water. I went under. There was a roar of water in my ears. My lungs felt as though they would burst. Then I came to the surface. I was alive, marvellously alive.' Kelly returned to work seventeen days later wearing new shoes, his old ones victims of the estimated 100 km/h impact with the water.

January 1932

A difference of opinion

Bradfield and Dorman Long's Ralph Freeman had a good working relationship; however, on a personal level, they clashed over who should be credited with designing the bridge. Initially played out in *The Sydney Morning Herald*, the disagreement reached a more intense level as the bridge neared completion when Dorman Long threatened to sue the Government of New South Wales if a plaque placed on the bridge named Bradfield as designer.

While Bradfield had set out the specifications for the tenders, Freeman, according to the terms of the contract, had been responsible for the working drawings, which, in turn, were checked by Bradfield. Bradfield had final word on all matters relating to the bridge. It could be argued that if the bridge had fallen down he would have worn the blame. He certainly took criticism for the decorative pylons at either end of the arch. Freeman made the point that he had started work on an arch design even before it was included in the tender documents. A plaque on the bridge reads, in part: 'The general design and specification were prepared and the whole supervised on behalf of the Government of New South Wales by J.J.C. Bradfield, D.Sc. (Eng.), M.E., M.Inst. C.E.,

M.I.E., Aust., Chief Engineer . . . Ralph Freeman, M.Inst. C.E., M. Am. Soc., C.E., Consulting and Designing Engineer for the Contractors.' The plaque also credits Lawrence Ennis, Dorman Long's Director of Construction.

There is no doubt that with his thirty years involvement in the on-again off-again project, both at the political and engineering level, Sydney Harbour Bridge exists as it does because of Bradfield; however, Freeman's contribution by way of the detail of this iconic and long lasting structure should not be diminished.

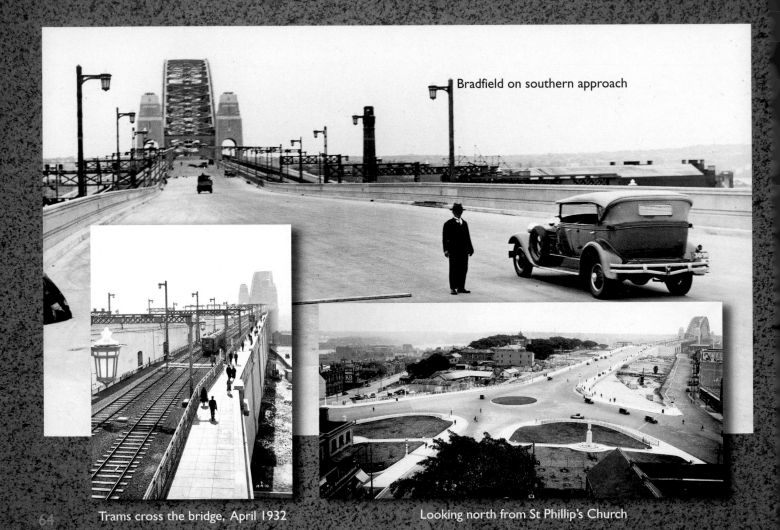

Bradfield on southern approach

64

Trams cross the bridge, April 1932

Looking north from St Phillip's Church

An uninvited guest at the opening ceremony

The official opening celebrations commenced at 10 am on a sunny Saturday 19 March 1932. The Governor initiated proceedings by reading a message from King George V. Premier Jack Lang, who was to officially open the bridge by cutting a wide blue ribbon, spoke next. It was just after Lang's speech that Francis de Groot, a native of Ireland and a captain in the New Guard, a right wing organisation opposed to the opening of the bridge by anyone other than a member of the Royal Family, or the Governor at least, etched his name in Australian folklore. De Groot, wearing a military uniform and riding a horse, had managed to get onto the bridge unchallenged. Seizing the moment, he charged the ribbon with his sword and cut it, crying out, 'On behalf of the decent and loyal citizens of New South Wales, I now declare this bridge open.' De Groot was pulled from his horse and arrested while a spare ribbon was located and stretched across the bridge. When Premier Lang cut this ribbon using the gold-plated scissors with inlaid opals presented to him by Dorman Long, a signal was sent triggering an artillery salute and an aeroplane flypast.

A procession of bridge workers, lifesavers, scouts, returned servicemen and colourful floats crossed the bridge as flag-decked ships sailed underneath sounding their sirens and horns. The first passenger train crossed the bridge to the cheers of onlookers and a temporary post office sold commemorative stamps. That evening saw special balls and dinners across Sydney and a Venetian carnival on the water, the highlight of which was a grand display of fireworks from Kirribilli Point and Fort Denison. At midnight, the bridge was opened to a line of vehicles stretching back two kilometres on the north side and to Sydney Town Hall on the south. During the next twenty-four hours, 25,000 vehicles paid the toll and crossed the bridge. Early the next month, with most of the country morning the death of the much loved racehorse Phar Lap, Francis de Groot was fined £5 for offensive behaviour in a public space and £4 costs.

Police officer arrests de Groot   Premier Jack Lang   65

Grandpa took it in stride

In 1931, Dr Bradfield escorted a small party of family members, including his first granddaughter, nine-year-old Shirley, onto the bridge deck and nonchalantly invited them to join him in a climb to the top of the arch. Shirley, now in her eighties, remembers walking unsteadily on the rivets, fighting her anxiety over the dizzying height until it all became too much and she asked to be taken back down. On 19 March the next year, young Shirley was with her parents as part of the official party at the bridge opening. Seated not far behind her grandfather and Premier Jack Lang, she laughed when she saw the commotion surrounding the Francis de Groot incident and was spoken to by her mother right there and then. 'And Granny was very cranky because of what de Groot did,' Shirley says now, 'but Grandpa took it in stride. He was a very humble, dignified man, a terrific grandfather. He would give me books and always asked me later how I'd enjoyed them and what they were about.' Shirley went on to work for the Bank of New South Wales and, in 1943, married an Australian army officer, Russell Fox, who later became a lawyer.

In 2003, Shirley was invited to cut the ribbon opening the new Pylon Lookout museum using the very same gold-plated scissors used by Premier Lang in 1932. Much to Shirley's surprise, when the moment came, the scissors would not cut through the ribbon; they were blunt. After some searching, a less impressive, but sharper pair was found to do the job.

Shirley Bradfield, age nine, with grandparents, uncle, father and aunt, September 1931

When The Rocks was The Rocks

Harry Lapham was born in working class Gloucester Street, The Rocks in January 1915, a time when tourism was almost unheard of and many of the businesses now occupying the neat rows of terrace houses could not have been imagined. A resident of the area his entire life, Harry says he grew up in a time 'when The Rocks was The Rocks'. He was a student at Fort Street Public School when the demolitions started and the bridge approach inched northwards, dwarfing everything below. He was delivering newspapers on the afternoon of 3 November 1927 when the signal master on Observatory Hill called out to him with news of the *Greycliffe* ferry disaster. Despite watching from boyhood to youth as the bridge took shape, Harry missed the opening ceremony. He went instead to rugby league trials at Moore Park where, much to his delight, he was selected for the Balmain reserve grade team. Not to miss out on the excitement entirely, that evening, he and some friends crossed the bridge on the pedestrian walkway taking in the fireworks and light displays from the ships in the harbour. For many years after the bridge opening The Rocks maintained its working class character. A plan to level the area for redevelopment in the early 1970s was thwarted by workers who made their living from demolition and construction: builder's labourers. Their union, the New South Wales Builders Labourers Federation under the leadership of Jack Mundey, made international headlines by imposing what they called a Green Ban on the modernisation project. Although the Rocks today is not The Rocks of Harry's youth, legislation ensures its unique character will be preserved for the enjoyment of generations to come.

Toll collection, April 1932. Sixpence (five cents) per car, threepence per horse and rider, a penny per head of sheep

April 1932

Stresses on the bridge

Gravity is not the only force accommodated in the bridge design. Strong wind acting on such a large surface produces a significant twisting force as does uneven loading of the deck. The design allows for gales much stronger than the most severe recorded in the area, 190 km/h, and stresses due to uneven loading and train and traffic movement were well tested prior to the bridge opening. Interlocking finger expansion joints at each end of the road deck and special joints in the railway lines allow for the six millimetre change in length with each degree Celsius change in temperature. Wedged in by the bearings, the arch bends as temperature changes and is about 180 mm higher at the hottest time of the year than at the coldest. Thermal and mechanical movement in the bridge is accommodated in pins and bearings which are regularly inspected and protected from wear by lubricants.

Making it last

Although the generally accepted life expectancy of steel structures is 100 years, with good care and maintenance, Sydney Harbour Bridge can be made to last indefinitely. The piers are in excellent condition and the steel, originally coated with red lead paint beneath the grey, has survived the years with little corrosion. Approximately eighty-five people work on the bridge and, contrary to popular belief, painters don't start at one end and work their way across just in time to start over. Some metal members get little exposure to the elements and can last up to thirty years before intervention is necessary, while others require spot repairs every five or so years. The major maintenance project over the next several years is the abrasive blasting of all metal on the southern approach followed by applications of epoxy zinc primer, epoxy micaceous iron oxide, and RTA Bridge Grey polyurethane. This project requires the erection of massive platforms and curtains to encapsulate the working space. A far cry from the early days when work was carried out in the open, painters now wear protective clothing and breathing apparatus

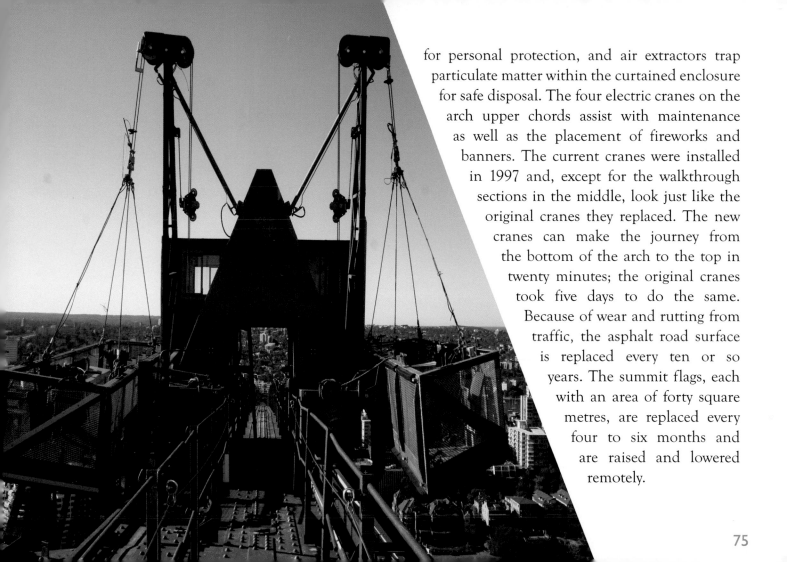

for personal protection, and air extractors trap particulate matter within the curtained enclosure for safe disposal. The four electric cranes on the arch upper chords assist with maintenance as well as the placement of fireworks and banners. The current cranes were installed in 1997 and, except for the walkthrough sections in the middle, look just like the original cranes they replaced. The new cranes can make the journey from the bottom of the arch to the top in twenty minutes; the original cranes took five days to do the same. Because of wear and rutting from traffic, the asphalt road surface is replaced every ten or so years. The summit flags, each with an area of forty square metres, are replaced every four to six months and are raised and lowered remotely.

75

Beyond Bradfield's wildest dreams

As the opening day loomed, one young man set his mind on collecting a unique souvenir that, unknowable to him, would, six decades later, play a significant part in a new life for the bridge, one neither Bradfield nor Freeman could ever have imagined: BridgeClimb. George Skinner was in his teens when he camped at the ticket office for two days in order to buy the first ticket for a seat on the first public train across the bridge. And George must have saved his pennies; at ten shillings, the souvenir ticket cost twenty times the toll for a motor vehicle. On opening day, to the cheers of those celebrating on the bridge deck, the first train, with a wide-eyed George on board, made its way slowly across the bridge to Milsons Point. A few minutes later it returned to Wynyard at normal operating speed. Many years later, George willed his treasured ticket to a fellow bridge enthusiast, his son-in-law, Paul Cave. Ticket 00001 would see Paul travel an entirely different journey.

In 1989, Paul Cave, by then a successful businessman, was involved in planning the World Congress of the Young Presidents' Organization held in Sydney that year. A number of participants in the congress, including Paul, had the privilege, seldom granted by the Roads and Traffic Authority, of climbing the bridge. Paul was so captivated by the experience that he set himself the goal of developing a public bridge climb within two years. Unfortunately, the New South Wales bureaucracy did not share his enthusiasm, their main concerns being the interference public climbers would pose to bridge maintenance and the possibility of a climber causing a terrible accident on the bridge deck. As an illustration, State Rail Authority of New South Wales regulations required anyone within five metres of a railway line outside a station to wear an orange reflective safety jacket. The proposed bridge climb had harnessed climbers descending a caged ladder within five metres of passing trains. Clearly, safety jackets were unnecessary and would distract motorists elsewhere on the bridge, but a rule is a rule and an exemption for BridgeClimb took two years to obtain. Paul's nine years of perseverance paid off on 1 October 1998 when he sent the first of what would be millions of bridge climbers on their way.

The climb experience

While the climb itself is the main event, the preparation, with its emphasis on safety, is a fascinating and enjoyable part of the three-and-a-half-hour experience. All potential climbers, including the group climb leader, must register below 0.05 on a breathalyser test before commencing. Since any item dropped during the climb could cause an accident below, watches and other loose items must be removed and, along with the contents of pockets, placed inside a locker. BridgeClimb staff issue each climber with a breathable, waterproof climb suit to be worn over regular clothing, or less if the day is warm. The two-tone grey of the suit blends with the grey of the bridge and minimises distraction to motorists. Depending on the weather and time of day, climbers may be provided with special headwear, a headlamp, gloves, a fleecy jacket or waterproof jacket and pants. Sunglasses or prescription glasses are attached to the suit by lanyard. And since not even a loose tissue is allowed on the bridge, handkerchiefs with wrist elastic are provided.

Once safety harnesses and headpiece radio receivers are fitted, the climb group, normally consisting of twelve people, undertakes a short simulator climb to get a feel for the ladders and catwalks on the bridge. Then, a short walk and a flight of stairs takes the group to the start of the catwalk under the southern approach where safety harnesses are attached to the static line, not to be removed until returning.

Climb leaders spend three months training before taking groups on their own and are encouraged to do their own research on the bridge to supplement what is provided in the course. Consequently, their commentaries are interesting, informative, and sometimes entertaining, and climb leaders are able to answer just about any bridge or local history question thrown at them by a group member. If they can't, they can radio base headquarters for help.

Deep-tread ladders take climbers through the deck at the southern pylon and onto the eastern upper chord of the arch for the gentle ascent to the top. Pacing the climb to suit the group, the climb leader stops when necessary to point out an interesting feature or take

individual or group digital photographs. Whether at dawn, dusk, daytime or night, the climb to the arch summit, 134 m above the water, is rewarded with, arguably, the most spectacular city view in the world. Then, with the traffic humming seventy-five metres below, climbers cross the catwalk to the western chord for an equally spectacular descent to earth.

Almost a quarter of a million people climb the bridge each year, eighty percent of these are visitors to Sydney. BridgeClimb employs about 260 people, 120 of whom are climb leaders. BridgeClimb has a sixty million dollar, twenty year lease on the part of the bridge it uses and pays a royalty to the government on every ticket sold; the funds generated are marked for bridge maintenance. There are 1439 stairs in the climb route. On average, three couples become engaged every week on the bridge, the ring being passed using a special BridgeClimb ERD, engagement ring device. Climbers must be at least ten years of age. There is no maximum age; the record is held by a a 100 year old woman.

200 STEPS TO THE TOP

The Pylon Lookout offers spectacular views
of the bridge, the harbour and the city.

Displays on all levels provide a unique insight
into the past and present of Sydney's celebrated
Harbour Bridge. Special features include a big
screen audio visual show presented in one of
the towering chambers of the pylon.

Adults	$8.50
Children (8-12 years)	$3.00
Children (7 years & under)	Free

Open 7 days, 10am to 5pm

A museum with a view

In 1934, the southeast pylon of Sydney Harbour Bridge was opened to the public. Reaching eighty-seven metres above mean sea level, the pylons were the tallest structures in Sydney at the time, fifteen metres higher than the next tallest, the tower at Central railway station, and twenty-five metres higher than the nearby Sydney Observatory time ball tower. Visitors in those days were treated to various amusements inside the hollow pylon and, outside, could take in views from the Blue Mountains to the Tasman Sea. In 1942 the pylon was taken over by the military and anti-aircraft guns were installed on the lookout. Four years after the war ended, a new operator established an exhibition inside celebrating the Australian way of life, installed coin-operated binoculars on the lookout, and sold kittens, the offspring of the dozens of white cats that roamed the premises. The operator and her cats found themselves on the street in 1971 when the Main Roads Department terminated the lease. The Roads and Traffic Authority reopened the pylon in 1982 as a museum featuring photographs and stories of the bridge under construction. In 2000, as part of their agreement with the government, BridgeClimb took over the operation of the pylon, restored it inside, built a small theatre and installed exhibits relating to the history and engineering of the bridge. As an ongoing project, the Pylon Lookout is compiling an Honour Roll to celebrate the achievement of all workers on the bridge project from engineer to day labourer.

Facts, figures and trivia

Final cost of bridge and approaches including property resumptions: £10 million ($300 million in today's money allowing for 3.5% inflation over eighty years)

1932 tolls: 6 pence (5 cents) for motor cars and motorcycles with side cars; 3 pence for sulkies, buggies, horse and rider, bicycle or motorcycle; 1 shilling (10 cents) for vans, lorries and wagons over 2 ton; 2 pence per head of cattle; 1 pence per head of sheep. The bridge was paid off in 1988. Bridge toll revenue now goes towards paying for the Sydney Harbour Tunnel. The tunnel loan should be paid off in 2023.

Length, width, and weight of arch: 503 m, 49 m, 39,000 t. In terms of span, width, and load carrying capacity, it is the greatest steel arch bridge in the world

Total length including approach spans: 1149 m

Height of top of arch above mean sea level: 134 m

Height of aircraft beacon (Blinky Bill) above mean sea level: 141 m

Headway for shipping below neon beacon at high water: 52 m

Height of pylons above mean sea level: 87 m

Thrust on each bearing: 20,000 t, 2.0×10^8 N

Steelwork: 53,000 t, 80% made by Dorman Long, 20% made by BHP and Australian Iron and Steel

Volume of concrete used: 95,000 m³

Volume of granite facing: 18,000 m³

Surface area of steelwork: 485,000 m² or 48.5 ha

Volume of paint per coat: 30,000 L (270,000 L was required for three coats during construction)

Thermal expansion allowance: Thermal forces pushing against the bearings can cause the arch to change in height by 180 mm over the seasons. There is a 420 mm allowance for expansion of the deck

Rivets: between 5 and 6 million, manufactured by McPhersons of Melbourne, varying in length from 32 mm to 370 mm, with a total weight of 3200 t

Crossings in first year including passengers and pedestrians: 29 million

Annual vehicular traffic: First 12 months: 7 million; 1950: 12 million; 1960: 28 million; 1970: 47 million; 1980: 58 million; 1990: 66 million; 2000: 59 million; Current: 64 million (Sydney Harbour Tunnel opened in 1992)

Vehicle accidents and breakdowns on bridge per annum (3 year average): 300; 3300

Tyne Bridge in Newcastle, England, a 162 m long metal arch bridge built by Dorman Long is commonly thought to be the model for the much larger Sydney Harbour Bridge. This is not the case. The contract for Tyne Bridge was signed after that for Sydney Harbour Bridge.

In 1931, workers reported a wailing sound on the bridge which they attributed to a bridge ghost. The sound was initially explained by engineers and scientist in terms of hollow metal reverberation caused by wind, much like the operation of organ pipes. When the sound continued on still days another explanation was sought. The sound seemed greatest on days with a large variation in temperature prompting the experts to explain it in terms of vibration caused by slipping in the expansion joints as the metal expanded.

During the years of construction, the future name of the bridge, commonly referred to as the North Shore Bridge, was subject to some debate. One letter to the editor of *The Sydney Morning Herald* suggested the bridge be called The Rainbow Bridge and the arch be painted the colours of the rainbow instead of drab grey.

In October 1931 a group of twenty bishops and archbishops wrote to Premier Lang criticising the choice of Holy Week, the week before Easter, for the bridge opening celebrations. That week was chosen to coincide with the Royal Agricultural Show.

Charlie Bell, a member of the New South Wales Amateur Swimming Association, offered to lend his talents to the opening ceremony by diving off the top of the bridge. His generous offer was declined.

Upon hearing that toll collectors were receiving electric shocks when accepting coins, Bradfield suggested they stand on rubber mats to insulate themselves from the earth and thereby prevent the discharge of static electricity through their bodies.

Bradfield went on to build his cantilever bridge, Brisbane's Story Bridge, which opened in 1940.

In October 1943, as onlookers held their breath, twenty-three-year-old Flight Lieutenant Peter Isaacson flew a Lancaster bomber under the bridge. Isaacson, who had just completed a hair-raising tour of duty in Europe, piloted the aircraft from England on a war bond promotion mission.

Trams ceased to run on the bridge in 1958, the space the lines occupied becoming lanes 7 and 8 of the Bradfield Highway in 1959.

In June 1973, French highwire artist Philippe Petit stopped traffic on the bridge with a performance on a wire he and friends had stretched between the northern pylons the night before. When police moved to cut the stabilising ropes attached to the wire, Petit hurried backwards to safety and arrest.

Paul Hogan, internationally famous as film character Crocodile Dundee, held down a day job in the early stages of his acting career. Paul was a rigger on Sydney Harbour Bridge.

Acknowledgements

Thanks to Peter Fenoglio to whom credit for the artistic design and layout of the book must go; BridgeClimb and staff for a spectacular afternoon and evening on the bridge; staff of State Records New South Wales for helping with access to the many historic photographs; staff of New South Wales Roads and Traffic Authority for answering my many questions and providing the opportunity to photograph from the north side of the bridge; Art Gallery of New South Wales, National Gallery of Victoria, Queensland Art Gallery and Ann Mills for permission to photograph the paintings by Grace Cossington Smith; Geoff Cooke and David Frieder for allowing the use of their magnificent African and American bridge photographs; Shirley Fox for sharing memories of her grandfather; Harry Lapham for sharing his stories of The Rocks; Takafumi Kato of Dynamic Helicopters; Elizabeth, Jenny and Peter Burchfield, Glenn Cooke, Wendy Cush, Karen Fenoglio, Denis Frisby, Darelle and David Housden, Carradine Lucas, Kate McDonald, Bernadette Moy and Max Salmon. Sources include *The Sydney Morning Herald*, 1900-1932; *The Commonwealth Engineer*, March 1932; *Main Roads*, March 1982; *The Story of the Sydney Harbour Bridge*, Department of Main Roads, New South Wales, 1982; *The Sydney Harbour Bridge, a life*, Peter Spearritt, 1982; *The unreasonable man: the life and works of J.J.C. Bradfield*, Richard Raxworthy, 1989; *The Bridge, the epic story of an Australian icon – the Sydney Harbour Bridge*, Peter Lalor, 2005.

Photo credits

BridgeClimb: pages 76 ticket background, 77, 77 inset, 78, 81; **James Burchfield:** pages 6-7; **City of Sydney:** pages 91, 92, 95 background; **Geoff Cooke:** page 23, Victoria Falls Bridge, *The Trans de Luxe crossing the bridge in the 1980s*; **Courtesy of Shirley Fox:** pages 19, 66; **David Frieder:** page 22, Hell Gate Bridge; **Michael Moy:** front cover, pages 1, 2, 3, 4, 5, 9, 10-11, 10 inset, 12, 13, 14-15, 15 inset, 18, 25, 31, 49, 53, 68, 69 inset, 71, 72, 73, 74, 75, 79, 79 inset, 80, 82, 83, 84, 85, 86, 88-89, 90, 94, 96 bottom, back cover left, background bridge steelwork, pylon granite, Sydney sandstone; **Newspix/News Ltd:** p 65 left; **North Sydney Council:** page 87, photographer: Gabrielle Green; **State Records New South Wales:** Department of Public Works; NRS 12685_a007_a00704_ prefixes all; page 8: 8725000001; p.12 inset: 8729000156; p.17: 8725000004; p.24 sketch; p.26: 8722000072; p.27: 8728000031; p.28: 8722000096; p.29: 8727000131; p.30: 8726000200; p.32: 8726000128; p.34: 8727000170; p.35: 8727000091; p.36: 8727000185; p.38: 8726000084; p.39: 8727000138; p.40: 8728000038; p.41: 8728000054; p.43: 8728000103; p.44: 8728000166; p.45: 8728000190; p.46: 8729000061; p.47: 8729000142; p.48: 8730000039 and 8729000143; p.50: 8730000033; p.52: 8730000050; p.54: 8730000078; p.56: 8730000115; p.57: 8731000008; p.58: 8735000073; p.60: 8723000128; p.62: 8733000117; p.63; p.64: 8724000150 top, 8724000163 left, 8724000155 right; p.65: 8734000190 right; p.67: 8723000147; p.69: 8724000151; p.70: 8724000153; p.96: 8733000020 top; back cover: 8729000156 right

First published in Australia by:
Alpha Orion Press
P.O. Box 207
Ashgrove QLD 4060
Australia
michaelmoy2001@hotmail.com

Graphic Design: Peter Fenoglio

Printed in China by Bookbuilders

Dedicated to good friends, Elnora and Glenn

National Library of Australia
Cataloguing-in-Publishing Data

Moy, Michael
Sydney Harbour Bridge : idea to icon

ISBN 0 9581066 4 9

1. Bridges, Arched - New South Wales - Sydney.
2. Sydney Harbour Bridge (Sydney, N.S.W.). I. Title.

624.22099441

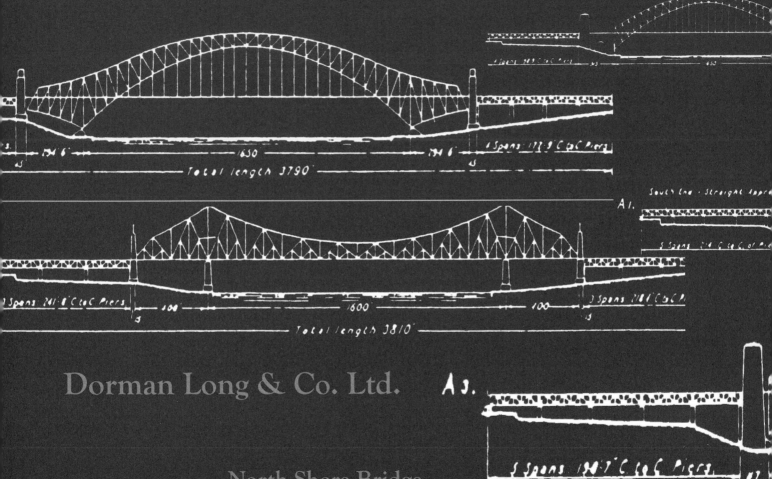

Total length 3790'

Total length 3810'

Dorman Long & Co. Ltd.

North Shore Bridge